Let's look at
HANDS

First published in 2001 by Zero To Ten Limited
327 High Street, Slough, Berkshire, SL1 1TX
This edition published under license from Zero To Ten Limited.
All rights reserved.

Copyright © 2001 Zero To Ten Limited
Text copyright © 2001 Simona Sideri
Illustrations copyright © 2001 Sheilagh Noble

Publisher: Anna McQuinn, Art director: Tim Foster, Publishing
assistant: Vikram Parashar

Published in the United States by Smart Apple Media
1980 Lookout Drive, North Mankato, Minnesota 56003

U.S. publication copyright © 2005 Smart Apple Media
International copyright reserved in all countries. No part of
this book may be reproduced in any form without written
permission from the publisher.
Printed in China

Library of Congress Cataloging-in-Publication Data

Sideri, Simona.
Hands / written by Simona Sideri ; illustrated by
Sheilagh Noble.
p. cm. — (Let's look at)
Summary: Children introduce the variety of hands and similar
appendages found in the animal kingdom and describe how
they are used.
ISBN 1-58340-493-7
1. Hand—Juvenile literature. 2. Extremities (Anatomy)—
Juvenile literature. 3. Anatomy, Comparative—Juvenile literature. [1. Hand. 2. Extremities (Anatomy).
3. Animals. 4. Anatomy.] I. Title: Let's
look at hands. II. Noble, Sheilagh, ill.
III. Title. IV. Let's look at (North
Mankato, Minn.)

QM548.S465 2004
571.3'1—dc22   2003058961

9 8 7 6 5 4 3 2 1

Let's look at
HANDS

Written by
Simona Sideri

Illustrated by
Sheilagh Noble

Hands are amazing!

How many fingers do they have?

How many thumbs?

A mole's front paws have long, broad nails.

They are
excellent for digging!

Bears have paws
with very long claws.

They are good for hunting
and catching food.

Seals use their flippers like paddles to swim.

On land their walk is more of a waddle.

Bats and birds
and other flying things
soar into the sky on their
wonderful wings.

Octopuses' tentacles
are long and thin.
They stretch out
to pull in prey.

The suckers underneath
the tentacles help them
grab onto rocks
and hold on tight.

Elephants use their trunks like hands!

Hands are **handy!**

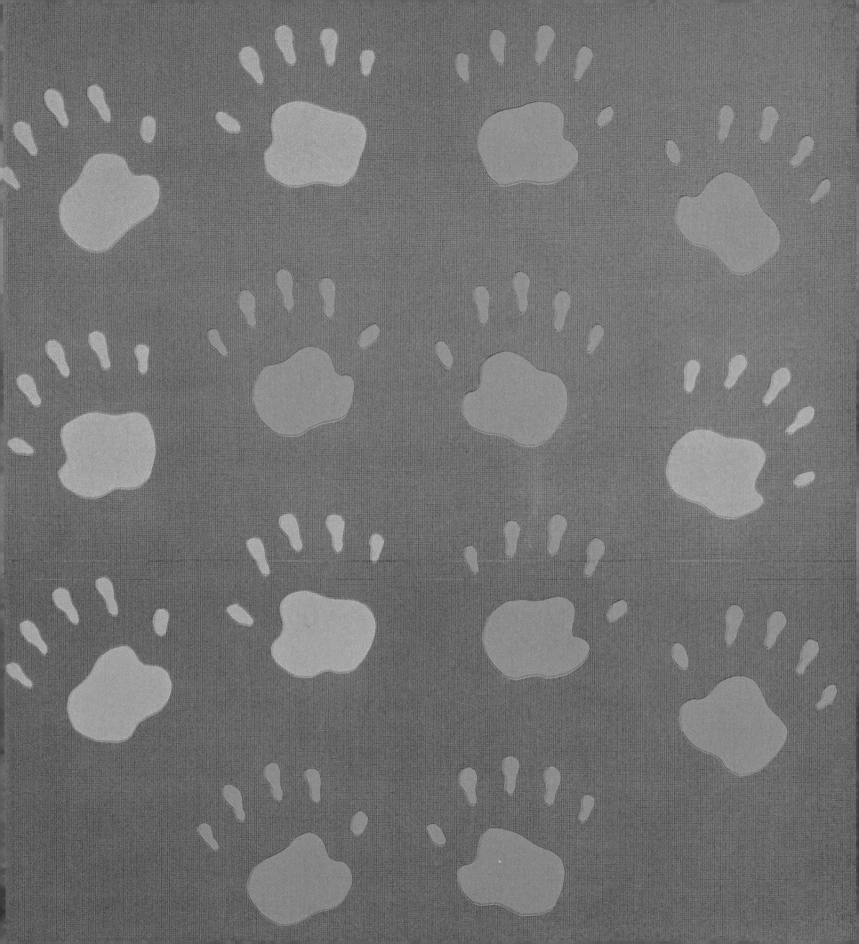

ML   N/04